CARDBOARD CITI

CaTHy

ALI TAYLOR

DIRECTED BY ADRIAN JACKSON

PREMIERE UK TOUR
OCTOBER 2016–FEBRUARY 2017

cardboard
citizens
25 YEARS

Supported using public funding by
ARTS COUNCIL
LOTTERY FUNDED   ENGLAND

LOTTERY FUNDED

CARDBOARD CITIZENS PRESENTS

CaTHy

ALI TAYLOR

DIRECTED BY ADRIAN JACKSON

Cathy was originally written to be performed as part of a Forum Theatre production.

Cathy was first performed at the Pleasance Theatre, London on 11 October 2016 as part of a UK tour.

CAST

CATHY	**Cathy Owen**
DANIELLE	**Hayley Wareham**
ALL OTHER FEMALE ROLES	**Amy Loughton**
ALL MALE ROLES	**Alex Jones**
UNDERSTUDY	**Carrie Rock**

JOKERS

Adrian Jackson, Terry O'Leary, Kerry Norridge

CREATIVE TEAM

Designer	**Lucy Sierra**
Lighting Designer	**Mark Dymock**
Sound Designer	**Matt Lewis**
Video/Digital Designer	**Edward Japp**
Assistant Director	**Emilia Teglia**
Dramaturg	**Sarah Woods**
Researcher	**Alison Cain**
Voice Coach	**Tim Charrington**
Casting Agent	**Sooki McShane & Lucy Jenkins**
Producer	**Emma Dunstan**
Assistant Producer	**Nick Gibson**
Production Manager	**Ed Borgnis**
Stage Manager	**Fergus Waldron**
Deputy Stage Manager	**Jasmin Hay**

All information correct at time of going to print

DIRECTOR'S NOTE

In 1966, Ken Loach's ground-breaking film, *Cathy Come Home*, outraged its audiences, with its depiction of a world unknown to many, and inspired a generation of activists and organisations to campaign for better housing and rights for homeless people. In 1991, Cardboard Citizens was born, a theatre company employing a similar mix of carefully researched testimony and artfully crafted fiction to tell powerful stories from the world of homelessness, with the goal of stimulating much-needed debate and action. To mark respectively the film's 50th and our 25th birthdays, we commissioned Ali Taylor to write a Forum Theatre play imagining what a Cathy *de nos jours* might look like – to explore and give our audiences a chance to see what has changed and what has not. Like Ken Loach and his team, Ali and his key researcher, Alison Cain, spoke to people at the sharp end of homelessness in London and beyond. These included the many Members of Cardboard Citizens with their own stories of hardship, as well as hard-pressed housing staff at councils who find themselves in the invidious position of judge and jury when people 'present' as homeless (on the day of their evictions, usually), dispensing what limited resources they have to support people, the housing stock available to them having been drastically reduced by decades of 'right to buy'. This play is the result.

Happily, we no longer live in an age where children are brutally ripped away from their parents by stern-faced agents of the state and homeless people warehoused in segregated institutions little changed from the workhouses of the 19th century. Attitudes have changed, what was normal then would not be acceptable now; hostels, though still unsuitable for the length of stay which many have to endure, are better places; there is more understanding of the pressures facing homeless people. But sadly, as this play testifies, the realities of the housing game and its vicious dependence on 'market forces' mean that families are still driven out of stable communities and often end up separated, emotionally and geographically; the shortage of housing stock results in scapegoating and resentment, and warped perceptions of outsiders usurping local people's entitlement feed divisions in our society.

The endless bubble of housing speculation hollows out parts of our cities, especially London, driving the poor further and further out, literally marginalising them. The spectre of Rachmanism is back, with unscrupulous private landlords legally able to exercise almost unlimited power over their tenants in substandard accommodation. Social housing, for much of the post-war period considered a normal human right, an appropriate way to deal with a necessary responsibility of the state, has been shrunken and shunted sideways to the very housing associations set up in the wake of *Cathy Come Home* – and even they are now forced into the game of developing and selling so-called 'affordable housing' to subsidise their core functions. As for council housing, it is now the province only of the very neediest in our society, and to earn the 'right' to access it requires people to prove that need in competition with one another in a squalid race to the bottom. It is difficult to see how this circle can be squared without enlisting the public (and ultimately those in power) to change the terms of the debate about how we view housing in this country – and enact whatever changes of policy are needed to rectify the situation.

One purpose in our staging of Ali Taylor's powerful and tender portrait of a family dealing with these pressures is indeed to open our audience's eyes to what is going on all around us, and, as in *Cathy Come Home*, hopefully to stoke up an anger which might lead to change. In a Forum Theatre presentation, after showing the play to an audience which has a stake in the issues, a discussion ensues, as to what might be different – how, in particular, the protagonists of the play, in this case Cathy and maybe Danielle, might have dealt with the oppressions that confront them in other ways, to try to overcome their problems. This is in no way intended to suggest that they are responsible for their situation – rather it is a provocation to see how all of us, however little power we appear to have, might confront the powerful institutions and mind-sets that surround us, to bring about change.

It is a very generous act on a playwright's part to create a play suitable for Forum Theatre. At the same time as telling a story, s/he must create a locus which provokes its audience to take the stage and imagine another way of ending the story – without descending into the realms of fantasy or wish-fulfilment. Having created a world on stage, s/he must effectively invite others to destroy and reshape it. The audience members do not merely discuss their ideas – they physically take the stage, replacing the central character, and enact their ideas, which the other characters resist or collaborate with, according to the reality of their motivations – this 'intervention' is already a form of action, and the hope is that it is a prelude to the enactment of similar changes in 'real' life.

This is Ali Taylor's second play in this mode for Cardboard Citizens, and we look forward to reporting at a later date the thoughts, interventions and actions that it generates when it tours to homeless and non-homeless audiences in hostels, theatres and prisons across the country. As with *Cathy Come Home*, the text presented here will be interpolated with video and sound recordings of testimony and vox-pops to prove that what is presented in the play is not a sentimental fiction, rather a report from the front.

We are often led to believe that the stories we are told – the inevitability of the market, the inhumanity of human to human, that notion the poor are the agents of their own catastrophe – are the only stories. A Forum Theatre play like *Cathy* invites us to invent other, better stories.

Adrian Jackson, Artistic Director, Cardboard Citizens
September 2016

BIOGRAPHIES

ALI TAYLOR | Writer

Ali Taylor trained at the Royal Court Young Writers' Programme. His first play *Cotton Wool* at Theatre503 won the 18th Meyer Whitworth Award. Ali went on to be one of the winners of 'Metamorphosis08', a new play competition run by the Churchill Theatre, Bromley, for his play *Overspill*. It was performed at the theatre before transferring to Soho Theatre. His writing for young people includes two plays for Polka Theatre: *Sticks and Stones* and an adaptation of *The Machine Gunners* (shortlisted for the Brian Way Award). His work also includes *Conspiracy* (RWCMD/Gate); *Under My Skin* (Pegasus); *Fault Lines* (Hampstead) and his radio plays for BBC Radio 4 including *Eight Feet High And Rising* and *Cinders*.

ADRIAN JACKSON | Director

Adrian Jackson is the Founder, Director and Chief Executive of Cardboard Citizens. Adrian founded Cardboard Citizens in 1991 and since then he has directed over 30 productions for the company, devising and writing many of them including *Pericles* and *Timon* (with RSC), *The Beggar's Opera* (with ENO), *The Lower Depths* (with London Bubble), *Mincemeat* (winner of Evening Standard Award). He directed his own play, *A Few Man Fridays* at Riverside Studios in 2012, and Kate Tempest's *Glasshouse* in 2013. In 2013 he wrote and performed an intervention in Elmgreen/Dragset's installation *Tomorrow* at the V & A. Adrian also teaches the Theatre of the Oppressed methodology all over the world.

CAST

ALEX JONES | Male Roles
Alex Jones is best known for his role as Clive Horrobin in the long running BBC Radio 4 Contemporary drama *The Archers* and subsequently *Archers & Ambridge Extra*, as well as over 100 other radio plays including *Heartlands* with BBC Radio 4 producer Jane Marshall, *The Old Curiosity Shop* and *Albion Tower* (winner of the Gold Sony Award). Recently he played Keith Loader in BBC's *Doctors*, other television and film includes *Jane Eyre*, *Fourth Arm*, *The Specials*, *Birds of a Feather*, *Back Up, Boon & Hardcases*, *Faster, Harder, Longer* and the BAFTA nominated film *Rhubarb And Roses*. His theatre credits include William Shakespeare in *Shakespeare and Various Irish Extracts* for the University of Birmingham (dir. Gwenda Hughes); Pilate in *The Mysteries* at Coventry Cathedral for Belgrade Theatre (dir. Barry Kyle); Anu/Ur-Shanabi/Panon in *Gilgamesh* (dir. Claudette Bryanston); Katie and 30 Other Characters in *I'm a Minger* (dir. Amy Bonsall) and productions at Birmingham Repertory Theatre including George in *Of Mice and Men*, Lederman in *Swamp City*, Slothworm in *Ash Girl* and Boatswain/Adrian in *The Tempest*.

AMY LOUGHTON | All Other Female Roles
Amy Loughton's theatre credits include: *Dear Uncle*, *Neighbourhood Watch* (both Stephen Joseph Theatre/No 1 tour/59E59 New York); *A View from the Bridge* (Theatre by the Lake, Keswick); *Peter Pan* (New Vic, Stoke-on-Trent); *Women, Power and Politics* (Tricycle); *Nation* (National Theatre); *Apart from George* (Finborough); *Blueprint for Write by Numbers* (Bike Shed); Sergeant Jackson in *Almost Near* (Finborough); Theatre Café Festival (Company of Angels) and *The Killing of Sister George* (Dramatic Productions). Her film credits include British features *Crowhurst* (Great Point Media) and *Aux* (Evolutionary Films). TV credits include *Talking to the Dead* (Sky/Warp Films), *EastEnders*, *Holby City* and *Emma* (all BBC).

CATHY OWEN | Cathy
Cathy Owen's theatre credits include: *This Wide Night* (Clean Break, Soho Theatre UK tour); *The Last Valentine* (Almeida); *Silent Engine* (Pentabus; Fringe First winner); *Kolbe's Gift* (Leicester Square); *Edwina: A Cautionary Tale for Grown Ups* (The Stadsteatern, Stockholm/BAC); *Mother Courage and Her Children* (National Theatre of Wales); *A Chaste Maid in Cheapside* (Almeida UK tour); *Macbeth* (Ludlow Festival); *Shrew'd: Taming of the Shrew*, *The Tamer Tamed* (Arcola); *Marisol* (Southwark Playhouse). Her television credits include *The Bill* (TalkBack Thames); *Casualty*, *Crown Prosecutor* (BBC) and *The Life and Death of Philip Night* (YTV/Waller Films).

HAYLEY WAREHAM | Danielle
Hayley Wareham trained at the Oxford School of Drama. Work since graduating includes: *This Secret Life* (tour); *Strawberry Starburst* (Brockley Jack) and *Is This Rape: Sex on Trial* (BBC3). Hayley has just completed the Soho Theatre Writers' Lab.

CARRIE ROCK | Understudy
Carrie Rock trained with Clean Break Theatre Company. Theatre credits include: *Seventeen Minutes* (Soho); *Julius Caesar,* all female cast (Donmar Warehouse/St Ann's Warehouse, New York); *Pastoral* (Soho); *Girls Like That* (Unicorn); *Sweatbox* (Latitude Festival); *A Woman Inside* (Etcetera/Edinburgh Fringe Festival/Hens and Chickens); *Rise* (Old Vic Community Company). Film credits include: *I Used To Be Famous* (Superplex Films) and *Mothers Inside* (Barnados).

ABOUT CARDBOARD CITIZENS

Cardboard Citizens began life in 1991, in the Cardboard City which had sprung up in what was then called the Bullring in London's Waterloo (now the site of the IMAX cinema), and its longevity in the field has earned it the trust and respect of homeless people, theatregoers and funders alike. The first members of the company included a number of those shanty-town rough sleepers, along with hostel-dwellers, transvestites, rent-boys and street drinkers.

From these rough and authentic beginnings, Cardboard Citizens has pioneered the use of participatory arts and theatre in particular with homeless people. In those days, the occasional unused pottery wheel in the corner of a day centre was the only form of arts activity provided for homeless people. Nobody thought that participation in the arts could make a real difference in people's lives, leading to tangible, measurable outcomes in everything from wellbeing to employment, and ultimately providing a real social return on the investment made. Now the picture is very different – Cardboard Citizens has proven that theatre can be a uniquely powerful tool for engaging homeless people in a process of change, and for engaging general audiences to focus on the plight of those at the margins of our society.

Whether these stories are presented in a homeless hostel or on the stage of a London theatre or the living room of a private house, the telling of these stories starts a conversation about change. And how that change could be brought about, translating ideas shared on stage into the real world. At street level, engaging homeless people with interactive Forum theatre and workshops, supporting them afterwards with advice and guidance, Cardboard Citizens empowers the dispossessed to move forward in their lives. At a national level, Cardboard Citizens shows hidden Britain to all who care to look.

Past Cardboard Citizens productions include: Forum Theatre tours of Kate Tempest's *Glasshouse*, Sarah Woods' *Meta* and *Benefit*; the Evening Standard Theatre Award-winning site-specific *Mincemeat*, and 2016's acclaimed Community Ensemble staging of *Cathy Come Home* at the Barbican Theatre.

ABOUT FORUM THEATRE

Cathy was originally written for a Forum Theatre production, a technique that can be used to explore different outcomes to productions. After the play is performed, with the help of a facilitator called 'The Joker' the audience are encouraged to suggest different actions and outcomes for the narrative, helping to actively engage with the issues that the play presents. Cardboard Citizens is one of the world's leading Forum Theatre practitioners.

For the last 25 years Cardboard Citizens' flagship project – the Forum Theatre Tour – has offered the opportunity for excluded audiences to access exceptional theatre. Cardboard Citizens shows are performed by actors who have experience of homelessness and present recognisable themes of homelessness, family relationships, employment and health which affect many marginalised people.

The Forum Theatre Tour is key to the ongoing work of the company, and is the best tool Cardboard Citizens has for engaging new members, finding supporters and making new relationships by:

- Presenting plays performed by people who have experienced homelessness for homeless audiences in hostels, day centres and foyers

- Enabling excluded people to develop their skills and confidence through projects and workshops

- Supporting participants' practical needs in matters of housing, education, employment and health, and signposting career and personal development

- Working in prisons and youth offenders centres to support those at risk of homelessness and/or reoffending through re-engagement and participation

Find out more about Cardboard Citizens' work and sign up to receive regular newsletters at **www.cardboardcitizens.org.uk**

HOW TO SUPPORT CARDBOARD CITIZENS

Are you with us?

For 25 years Cardboard Citizens' pioneering and creative approach has supported some of society's most disadvantaged and neglected people. There are various ways you can support us, from core projects to seasons of work.

As a national charity we rely on the generosity and commitment of our friends and supporters for over 80% of our income – over £1 million every year. Without it, we simply wouldn't be able to deliver our outreach, educational and artistic programme of work.

The demand for our work is increasing every day, with more referrals than ever and the risk of homelessness in London at its greatest. In the past five years alone rough sleeping has risen by 55% in England, affecting young people and adults from every conceivable background.

Your support can and will have lasting impact.

Call 020 7377 8948 or visit www.cardboardcitizens.org.uk to donate.

CATHY

Ali Taylor

For Agnes

Acknowledgements

Thanks to all those people who gave up their time to be interviewed for this play: the Cathys living in temporary accommodation, especially Elina Garrick; housing officers at London councils; Phillippa Middleton, Valentina Ines La Mela and Bex Bellingham at The Marylebone Project; Kevin Garvey at Shelter; and Marc Francis at Z2K.

Thanks also to Lou Ramsden; Charlotte Knight and Rhia Douty at the Knight Hall Agency; and everyone at Cardboard Citizens.

Special thanks to director Adrian Jackson, researcher Alison Cain, dramaturg Sarah Woods, assistant director Emilia Teglia and stage manager Jasmin Hay, as well as the cast of Cathy Owen, Hayley Wareham, Amy Loughton and Alex Jones.

A.T.

Characters

CATHY, *forty-three*
DANIELLE, *fifteen, Cathy's daughter*

JAY, *thirty-seven, estate agent*
REG, *seventy-six, Cathy's dad*
SHANIA, *twenty-four, housing officer*
SAL, *forty-one, estate management*
GARY, *thirty-nine, estate management*
ANJA, *thirty-two, resident of Churchill House*
PETER, *fifty, senior housing officer*
BEX, *forty-four, Cathy's sister, Danielle's aunt*
GLEN, *forty-four, Cathy's ex-husband and Danielle's dad*
KAREN, *fifty-eight, bus driver*

The play can be performed with the following doubling:

Jay / Reg / Gary / Peter / Glen
Shania / Sal / Anja / Bex / Karen

Notes

/ indicates an interruption or quick response

– indicates where a sentence is stopped by the speaker

… indicates where a thought drifts away

[word] indicates the intended next word(s) in a sentence

Beat indicates a change of tone

This text went to press before the end of rehearsals and so may differ slightly from the play as performed.

Scene One

April 2015. CATHY's flat in East London. Evening.

JAY stands. He is dressed in a fashionable suit. CATHY is dressed casually, ready for her cleaning work. DANIELLE sits on the sofa with a textbook and exercise book open. She is dressed in school skirt and top, no tie. She is in the middle of homework.

JAY. Forty-three years!

CATHY. Forty-three years.

JAY. I can't believe that!

CATHY. Born and bred.

JAY. Born and bred.

CATHY. That's right. It's like I got this place in my veins.

JAY. Writ through you like rock.

CATHY. I know every street.

JAY. Course you do.

CATHY. The people, the caffs, the best pubs.

JAY. You ent always been in here?

CATHY. Ten years in this flat.

Moved out when I got married, back when my mum passed.

JAY. And very nice it is. Two bed, bathroom, balcony. Attractive views over the communal gardens. What is it, seven hundred square foot?

CATHY. I guess.

JAY. All them years round here, that's something. I've always moved around. Shepherd's Bush, Brixton, Hoxton, you know. But I came back, my mum called up said, 'Jay, we need you back in the fold, son.'

CATHY. Your mum alright?

JAY. Yeah yeah, the old girl's all cool. She's getting elderly now. All those years taking its toll. That's why I'm taking on the portfolio. So, I was in the area, I thought I'd drop in.

I appreciate it's unannounced and that.

CATHY. Your mum always gave us notice.

JAY. I do apologise, I do. I wanted to touch base.

CATHY. It's seven o'clock, Jay. I'm going out to work.

JAY. I promise I won't be long. I appreciate you gotta go.

(*To* DANIELLE.) And I can see you're in the middle of homework there. What is that, Physics or summin'?

DANIELLE. History.

JAY. Old days' stuff. You crack on with that. When I was at school the only A I got had the word 'detention' after it.

His joke dies.

Sorry, I should take my shoes off.

CATHY. I don't mind.

JAY. No, I hate it when people just walk the streets in. I don't want their footprints in my place. It's my home.

Home ain't just where the heart is. It's where my new carpets are too.

His joke dies. He places his shoes on the floor.

Can I call you Catherine?

CATHY. Or Cathy, Cath, whatever.

JAY. And you are?

DANIELLE. Too young for you.

JAY. Ha! I like that! Bants! Nice bants.

CATHY. Danielle.

JAY. Danielle, I'm Jay.

> JAY *holds out his hand.* DANIELLE *shakes it, reluctantly.*

> I don't wanna take up your time, Cathy. I wanted to check if you'd got our letters.

CATHY. Your letters?

JAY. Yeah yeah, just a couple of letters we sent.

CATHY. I don't know if I've seen any –

JAY. They was first class.

CATHY. Dan?

DANIELLE. In the hall?

CATHY. Maybe. I don't always check.

JAY. Things slip. I get that.

CATHY. I do keep on top of everything but I'm out ten, twelve hours a day.

JAY. You're a busy person, I can see that.

> (*For* DANIELLE*'s benefit.*) It's a very industrious place here.

> The letters were addressed to a Mr Glen Ward, is that your husband?

CATHY. Was.

JAY. Oh, I'm sorry, is he – ?

CATHY (*ruefully*). He is still alive. Sadly.

JAY. Is there any chance he could have opened them, taken them away?

CATHY. No.

DANIELLE. We chuck out his post.

CATHY. He walked out on us nine years ago. He ain't been back since. Nor will he be.

JAY. Okay cool. Just that… they're /

CATHY. My shift's in half an hour, Jay. I can't be late.

JAY. Just that… the letters are kind of important so, if you could find them. We do need to properly chat about 'em… sort of now… yeah.

CATHY. I might have put 'em in a drawer in the kitchen. I'll look.

JAY. Thank you, Cathy, that would be cool.

Exit CATHY. JAY *is left with* DANIELLE. DANIELLE *gets on with her homework. He doesn't know what to say or do. He looks out the window. Inspects the window frame, condition of the ceiling, all the time glancing at* DANIELLE. DANIELLE *feels this and picks up her phone and begins sending a message (about* JAY) *which makes him paranoid. He fetches his phone out of his suit jacket.*

That the iPhone 5 is it?

DANIELLE. 4.

JAY. This the 6. Nice, light, for the size.

DANIELLE *couldn't be less bothered.*

What's that you doing, chatting is it?

Snapchat? Instagram?

DANIELLE. Instagram.

JAY. I'm on Instagram. You could follow me. Or I could follow you.

DANIELLE *gives him a dismissive look.*

Nah, come on! I ent that old, am I?

DANIELLE. Are you?

JAY. Guess. Go on, guess how old I am.

DANIELLE. Forty?

JAY. Forty! Thirty-seven, man. I still got all my hair, yeah. Forty!

So what's that, A levels, is it?

DANIELLE. GCSEs.

JAY. No! You only sixteen?

DANIELLE. Fifteen.

JAY. Fifteen. I'd put you about eighteen, you know. Seriously.

GCSEs, eh. So you doing alright. I bet you pretty clever, innit?

Enter CATHY.

DANIELLE. Not really.

JAY. I can tell. All As, I bet. Yeah?

CATHY. Straight As.

DANIELLE. It's not gonna happen, Mum.

JAY. What you thinking: college, uni, that kind of thing?

DANIELLE. Yeah.

CATHY. Tell him what you wanna do.

DANIELLE. Mum!

CATHY. – ! Go on! Tell him!

DANIELLE. I wanna be a taxidermist.

JAY. Taxidermist? You want to drive a cab??

DANIELLE. Taxidermy is the practice of preserving animals. Mum says stuffing animals is weird /

CATHY. It is!

DANIELLE. If your Labrador dies, you should just get another dog.

JAY *crouches and whispers to* DANIELLE.

JAY. Mums don't always know what's best for us. My mum, she was like, 'Jay, you wanna go into law.' I was like, 'Nah, the future is property. That's where the profit is.'

That's why I got a beamer outside.

If your mum earned proper you wouldn't be in the trouble you're in.

DANIELLE. What do you mean? Mum, are we in trouble?

JAY *moves away from* DANIELLE.

CATHY. We're not in trouble.

What have you said to her?

JAY. Ah yeah, well it's sort of like…

Those letters were demands. For rent arrears.

CATHY. We're behind a bit. Your mum knows I'll make it up.

JAY. Cathy? You owe three months' rent. That's eighteen hundred pound. We kinda need that money.

CATHY. But your mum said –

JAY. Like I say, she's elderly, she's let a lot of things slip so –

CATHY. I told her, I've had my shifts cut at work, we're all on zero hours now. And I just ent earning enough at the moment. It'll pick up.

JAY. Get a loan, then? Make up the deficit next week?

CATHY. I've never been late before, Jay.

JAY. End of the month then.

See, I've just been in the block just over there. Handing the keys over to a nice young couple, young professionals. You know how much they were paying for the same unit? Two thousand five hundred a month.

How much do you think you pay? Four hundred and twenty-two from housing benefit. Six hundred from you.

Makes you think doesn't it?

DANIELLE. That those people are mugs?

CATHY. Dan!

JAY. It's alright, ha, that's very amusing.

When I get tenants in arrears, I get it in the neck from Dad. 'Don't let these people take the piss,' he says. 'Get 'em out.'

CATHY. But I lived on the estate all my life.

JAY. And you have a right to live here forever?

CATHY. This is my home.

JAY. No, no. It's my home. You rent it from me.

JAY *puts his shoes on.*

DANIELLE. I go to school here, all my mates are on the estate.

CATHY. Give me a month.

JAY *shakes his head.*

Your mum / let us owe her a month…

JAY. Sorry, that ain't gonna happen. World's changed.

Can you pay us what you owe, Cathy?

CATHY. Yes, I said.

JAY. Can you pay us what you owe, Cathy?

CATHY. –

JAY. I need to hear yes.

Can you pay us what you owe, Cathy?

CATHY. Yes.

JAY *takes a folder and opens it. He slides out a crisp headed letter.*

JAY. This is a Section 21 notice. It is addressed to you, Mrs Catherine Ward. I am putting it in your hand.

CATHY *takes the letter.*

It states that due to rent arrears we at Stereo Estates will terminate your tenancy on the fourteenth of May.

CATHY. You can't do that.

JAY. I don't want to, believe me.

You got fourteen days to pay. If you don't, you're gonna have to get out of my flat.

Scene Two

September 2015. A care home in East London. Late afternoon.

REG *sits in an armchair, watching* CATHY *and* DANIELLE. CATHY *is unpacking bought flowers and putting them in a vase.* DANIELLE *is scrolling through Rightmove on her phone.*

DANIELLE. You're not supposed to have liked it!

CATHY. I did like it!

DANIELLE. But not click like, Mum!

CATHY. It was lovely what you were saying about that boy. It was romantic.

DANIELLE. Now everyone's seen it and they're all like, 'Your mum thinks you fancy Charlie Baines.'

CATHY. Do you fancy him?

DANIELLE. A bit, but…

CATHY. Should I not like it then?

DANIELLE. No! Just move on.

CATHY. You've liked my pictures.

DANIELLE. One I did. You know Instagram ain't just for photos of your dinners.

CATHY. I was very proud of that lasagne.

REG. Who the fuck are you two?

CATHY. Cathy, Dad. It's Cathy.

REG. Cathy?

CATHY. See that photo? I'm the one in the middle.

REG. You're not Bex.

CATHY. She's your other daughter. The one who don't visit.

REG. You're Cathy?

CATHY. Yes I'm Cathy and that's Danielle, she's mine. (*To* DANIELLE.) Danielle, get off Snapchat and talk to your granddad.

DANIELLE. Actually I'm on Rightmove.

(*To* REG.) You got any wifi here yet, Granddad?!

CATHY. Don't ask him that.

REG. I've seen your face before but you – (*To* DANIELLE.) no.

Bex visits.

CATHY. Does she really?

REG. Every Tuesday and Thursday.

DANIELLE. It's Mum that visits you, not Bex, Granddad.

(*To* CATHY, *offering a picture on the phone*.) What about this one?

CATHY. That's far too much.

REG. How long you staying for?

CATHY. Not long. I've got to be gone by six.

REG. The butcher's don't open that late.

CATHY. You're thinking of Mum. She worked in the butcher's. I do cleaning. In Canary Wharf.

We're seeing a new flat at six.

REG. You're moving?

CATHY. We're being evicted.

REG. –

CATHY. Dan, pick up those clothes.

DANIELLE. Mum, they're his pants. Granddad, you don't want me touching your pants, do you?

REG. I don't know you.

CATHY *picks up the pants and puts them to one side.*

CATHY. I'm gonna have a word with Barbara. They should help you clean up.

REG. You tell her about the others. There's two of 'em who come in here when I'm asleep. And they steal things. One had my watch in his hand the other day. He sold it.

DANIELLE. It's here, Granddad.

REG. That's not my watch.

CATHY. Yes it is. It's the one your dad gave you.

REG. It's not. I've looked.

(*To* DANIELLE.) Go down round the pawn shops. Ask if they've seen a dusky man with my dad's watch.

When's your mum back?

CATHY. She's not, Dad.

REG. Is she with Cathy?

CATHY. No, she's not.

I'm Cathy, Dad.

REG. Cathy? My Cathy. Oh yeah, yeah. Sorry.

CATHY. It's alright. It's confusing, isn't it?

REG. I ent been sleeping too good.

Bird next door, sings. All night.

CATHY. But you alright otherwise, Dad? You taking your pills?
Your feet alright?

REG *shrugs his shoulders. He wiggles a foot.*

REG. This one not so much.

CATHY *sits next to him. And taps her thigh.*

CATHY. Put it here then.

REG *lifts his leg as high as he can.* CATHY *puts his foot on
her leg and massages his foot.*

REG. Did you say I'm being evicted?

CATHY. No, Dad, we are. We have to be out by the start of
October. We're looking for something else on the estate but
all the prices gone sky high.

REG. You can't live here.

DANIELLE. Ah no! Really? We're looking for somewhere that
smells of wee.

CATHY. Danielle!

DANIELLE. What?

CATHY. We'll find somewhere.

DANIELLE. We ain't gonna abandon you, Granddad.

REG. You ask the council?

CATHY. I did and they said they can't help us with a place until
we get kicked out.

REG. The council got us a flat.

CATHY. I know. That was before they sold them all off to
Stereo Estates. Things have changed since your day.

CATHY *continues massaging* REG's *foot.* DANIELLE *begins eating* REG's *grapes.*

How's that? Better?

REG *looks over to* DANIELLE.

REG. What's that you're eating? Little green bollocks.

DANIELLE. Grapes, Granddad.

CATHY. He knows!

DANIELLE *offers grapes to* REG. *He takes one.*

REG (*grins*). I like grapes. I'm not in hospital, am I?

CATHY. It's your room, Dad. In Cumbermere Lodge.

REG. I know. I live here. Full of old cunts in nappies.

All they do is sleep /

CATHY's *phone rings,* CATHY *takes the call. The following speeches overlap and cut into each other.*

CATHY. Hi – this is Cathy /

REG. You're being evicted from the estate?

DANIELLE. Yeah.

CATHY. We're coming at six – It's me and my daughter.

REG. I remember it being built. Great big blocks up into the sky.

CATHY. Fifteen.

REG. We all moved in together. You could leave your doors open /

CATHY. I'm a cleaner /

DANIELLE. And everyone knew each other?

CATHY. It's a contract.

REG. What are you laughing at? They did! And we had street parties.

DANIELLE. Once. In 1977.

CATHY. Housing benefit, yeah I do.

Hello? Hello?

CATHY *looks at the phone, takes stock.*

DANIELLE. Cancelled then?

CATHY. Yeah. No DSS again.

REG. No it's all changed now.

Pause.

DANIELLE. What if we don't find anywhere, Mum?

CATHY. We will.

REG. Everyone's out for number one.

DANIELLE. But if we don't –

CATHY (*snaps*). We just will alright –

Get your coat. There's an agent on Grove Street we haven't been to yet.

CATHY *picks up her coat and any bags she has with her.*

REG. You going?

CATHY. Yep, I'll see you on Thursday, Dad. I'll bring you dinner.

CATHY *puts her coat on.*

REG. Cath, where's your mum?

CATHY. She's gone away, Dad.

REG. Got Bex with her?

CATHY. Yeah, she has.

Scene Three

*October 2015. London borough of Thames Wick housing office.
Early evening.*

*A table with two chairs on either side. There is a Perspex
partition in the centre of the table (optional in staging).*

CATHY *is wearing her coat. She has set down the large bags
she has been holding.* DANIELLE *stands with a large suitcase
and rucksack and as many bags as she can carry. She is
anxious, scared.*

SHANIA, *a housing officer, is dressed in casual professional
clothes, carrying a folder of documentation.*

SHANIA. Mrs Ward.

    CATHY *starts to faint,* DANIELLE *goes to her.*

    Are you alright /

CATHY. It's just, my head, being in this building, there's no
    windows and /

SHANIA. Can I get you some water? /

CATHY. We've been waiting so long

    Out there and /

    This room, I feel like I have been arrested.

SHANIA (*to the corridor*). Are you okay?

CATHY. I'm alright.

SHANIA. Sure? Are you alright to carry on?

    They go to sit.

CATHY. I've never asked for anything, all these years.

    I said I wouldn't do benefits, cos I've always managed on
    my own.

    I've been working so hard…

    I want you to know I'm not a scrounger.

DANIELLE. She knows, Mum, alright.

CATHY *takes a couple of deep breaths*.

CATHY. Sorry.

SHANIA. Okay. Mrs Ward.

CATHY. Ms. It's Ms Ward.

SHANIA. Ms Ward.

CATHY. Sorry. Breathe. I gotta breathe.

They sit on the chairs.

SHANIA. I have to make a determination based on the information you given us in this form /

CATHY. Yeah yeah /

SHANIA. And decide whether we are in a position to help you or not.

CATHY. What do mean, 'not'?

SHANIA. I have to decide whether we have a duty of care to you or whether you have made yourself intentionally homeless.

DANIELLE. What? /

CATHY. Intentionally? Why would I do this on purpose?

SHANIA. I'm not saying you did.

CATHY. I did everything you people told me to do. I went to court, I challenged the Section 21. But he got his possession order. And at seven this morning, the bailiffs came and they took everything and piled it up on the pavement outside so all my neighbours could see /

SHANIA. I know /

CATHY. She's missed a day of school cos she was sat out there in the reception with all of our things. For nine hours.

DANIELLE. Mum! She knows.

SHANIA. I am aware of the circumstances.

CATHY. Sorry.

I don't want to ask for help but I need… they said you could get us a place to stay.

SHANIA. All I was saying is that we *could* find you intentionally homeless. If, for example, we found that you had ignored the Section 21 letter from your landlord. Or you did not take adequate steps to avoid rent arrears.

CATHY. I did, though, I work every hour I can. I was trying to make it up.

SHANIA. Ms Ward.

DANIELLE. Mum, you gotta chill.

CATHY. I don't like the suggestion I let this happen.

SHANIA. You have nowhere else to go? Family?

CATHY. My mum's dead. Dad's in a home.

I've got an ex, her dad, but he's a gambler so we ain't going there. And my sister but we don't speak so no, no one.

There's no savings, no pension.

Can you get us a place? It's six o'clock.

SHANIA *pauses for effect, preparing to manage* CATHY*'s expectations.*

SHANIA. Okay. If we decide that you are eligible for assistance then these are the facts. You have a dependent child so you are Band 2 and Priority Need. Under Article 8 of the Human Rights Act we have a duty to house you.

But.

We don't have enough properties in the borough.

We have two thousand people who want a temporary home.

CATHY. But we live here.

I've got three jobs, my dad's care home is round the corner. And she's got exams next year.

SHANIA. We can offer emergency accommodation.

You'll stay there while we investigate your circumstances. This assessment will take thirty-three days. If we decide you're eligible, then we'll move you into temporary accommodation.

CATHY. Thank you.

SHANIA *pushes the documentation towards* CATHY.

SHANIA. Churchill House. It's bed and breakfast.

CATHY *begins reading the documentation.* SHANIA *slides over the keys.*

CATHY. Luton?

DANIELLE. Where's Luton?

CATHY. That's not, we can't go to Luton.

SHANIA. It's only a month.

DANIELLE. How will I get to school?

SHANIA. There are trains to London.

It's an hour and a quarter to King's Cross. And then buses.

DANIELLE. That's three hours a day.

CATHY. And how much will that cost?

SHANIA. Not more than twenty pounds a day /

CATHY. That's a hundred pounds a week.

SHANIA. It's a studio with shared kitchen and bathroom.

CATHY. One room. Please, Shania, you must have something closer. It's her GCSEs.

SHANIA. This is our offer.

DANIELLE. Luton?

CATHY *pushes the documentation and keys back across the table to* SHANIA.

CATHY. Have you called around? There must be landlords round here with a spare room or something.

SHANIA. It's too late in the day.

CATHY. Give me some numbers, I'll call 'em.

SHANIA. We can't do that.

CATHY. I've paid my taxes all my life and I've never asked for help.

SHANIA. I am going to have to ask you to calm down. Or I'll have to call security.

CATHY. I am calm.

Please. Please.

Pause.

SHANIA. Look, we've made our offer. You are at liberty to arrange your own accommodation.

CATHY. I've tried that.

SHANIA. Well then.

CATHY. Pass me the keys.

SHANIA *pushes the keys across the table. And the documentation.* CATHY *signs the document.*

SHANIA. I'll get you a number for a taxi.

Scene Four

October 2015. Luton. A small room in Churchill House.
Morning.

A mattress with two duvets. Piles of possessions in boxes.
Drying clothes hanging up off the radiator, back of the door,
etc.

DANIELLE *is holding a takeaway Tupperware box with five*
cockroaches. CATHY *is in casual clothes.*

SAL *is dressed in a suit.* GARY *is dressed in a suit, on his*
hands and knees, using the flashlight on his phone to look into
the gap between the wall and floor.

CATHY. There were four.

DANIELLE. Five.

CATHY. In here.

DANIELLE. One got away.

CATHY. They were round our food.

GARY. When was this?

CATHY. That was the second night, wasn't it? The second night
we were in.

DANIELLE. Tuesday, I could hear them scratching.

GARY. And you saw one today?

CATHY. Coming out of there.

CATHY *points to the cracks between the wall and floor.*

SAL. See anything, Gary?

GARY. Not as yet.

CATHY. Show her, Dan. She kept them to show you.

DANIELLE *takes the box to* SAL *to show her.* SAL *recoils.*

GARY. We're not saying we don't believe you.

CATHY. Five though. That's an infestation, isn't it.

DANIELLE *offers the takeaway Tupperware box in* SAL*'s direction. She recoils.*

GARY *stands, dusts himself down.*

GARY. There's no sign of anything down here.

DANIELLE. Cockroaches can go half an hour without air. And live for a month without food.

SAL. Ridiculous.

DANIELLE. People say they live through nuclear bombs. They can't. It's a myth.

CATHY. Not now, Danielle.

DANIELLE. They can live without a head for a week. And they spread salmonella and polio.

CATHY. They're walking all over our food.

SAL. You got the lid pressed down tight?

DANIELLE. Yeah.

SAL *moves to the area in the space furthest from the cockroaches.*

GARY. We haven't had any other complaints.

CATHY. Really?

SAL. Your council's been putting people here last two years. We've had no issues. Most people put their head down, / try and settle.

GARY. Try and settle.

CATHY. We're not complaining, we wanted you to know. So you can get someone in, get rid of them.

SAL *and* GARY *look to each other.*

SAL. Right.

CATHY. So – ?

SAL. Well –

GARY. We don't know if they are [from here] –

SAL. We don't know if you found them in here? You could have brought them with you?

CATHY. With their own little suitcases?

GARY. ...picked them up on your way in.

SAL. No one else has ever complained.

DANIELLE. Erm – ?

SAL. You know how it looks from my side. I get no complaints. You arrive: they arrive.

CATHY. We didn't bring them.

SAL. You can't prove that.

GARY. We've heard it all you know. All the reasons why people need to move into a bigger room or better room. All sorts of excuses.

SAL. Can you not be touching that lid.

CATHY. We're not asking to move rooms.

DANIELLE. We sort of don't want polio.

SAL. We can't fit you in anyway. We're got a family of four today coming from Waltham Forest.

GARY. Thing is, you keep this place clean and tidy. That would stop any issues with pests.

CATHY. Oh my God, are you saying we made this dirty?

SAL. Look at the mould on that wall. That's black up there.

GARY. Get into your lungs that.

CATHY. You know that can't have been –

We've only been here a week.

SAL. So how have you managed that then?

CATHY. – ?

When we first got here, there was nothing in here, not even a
lightbulb. And even then you could see it was filthy. The bin
was full of rotting KFC.

DANIELLE. Like cockroach heaven.

CATHY. We was told this was a bed and breakfast. And there
was no bed. And there definitely weren't no breakfast.

GARY. The council do know it comes unfurnished.

CATHY. And no plates, fridge, nothing.

DANIELLE. We scrubbed this place top to bottom.

CATHY. I'm a cleaner.

SAL. Then you should know how to get this mould off.

GARY. I mean, you've got to keep these rooms ventilated.
Open these windows.

SAL. You can't keep all your clothes drying in here.

CATHY. There's nowhere else to put them.

SAL. There's the laundrette in town. It only takes a couple of
hours.

CATHY. But I work all day.

GARY. Look, we're only advising you.

SAL. You'll be in breach of your tenancy agreement if this falls
into disrepair.

GARY. You won't get a problem with pests if you keep this
place clean.

SAL. Wash up your plates. Don't leave all these crumbs around.

GARY. And don't pile all your stuff up against the walls.

Beat.

SAL. If there's nothing else?

GARY *holds out his hand to* DANIELLE.

GARY. I'll take those, young lady. I'll find them alternative accommodation.

DANIELLE *is about to give* GARY *the box. She withdraws the box.*

DANIELLE. Nah, you're alright, I'll deal with them.

Beat.

GARY. Have it your way.

SAL. Okay then?

GARY. Buy some powders and traps. If there's a problem in a fortnight, call us again. Yeah?

SAL. Maybe get a dustpan too?

Scene Five

January 2016. Luton. Oceans nightclub in Luton. The sound of muffled house music from inside. The fire door is held ajar with a brick.

CATHY *is dressed all in black.* ANJA *is dressed identically to* CATHY. *They are on a break.* ANJA *is excited and leads* CATHY *in singing and jumping along to the song from inside the club – Sia's 'Cheap Thrills'.*

CATHY *joins in with the song from time to time.*

The song continues in the background and later blends into another current pop song.

ANJA. Show me how much you got then.

CATHY *takes the money out of a pouch.* ANJA *counts it.*

CATHY. Not bad, eh!

ANJA. This is all?

CATHY. It's not enough?

ANJA. You should make twice this! This is bullshit money, Cathy. Have you *been* in bathroom? Are you speaking to them?

CATHY. Yeah, everything you said.

ANJA. Bullshit you are!

CATHY. I am!

ANJA. You are sit in corner picking your nails! I know it!

CATHY. Anja! I'm doing it like you said. Flip the tap on. Then squeezing the soap. Then offering the towel.

ANJA. And what you say? 'You look pretty tonight, your tits look like mountains, all man want you.'

ANJA begins lighting a cigarette.

CATHY. I'm too old for this, aren't I?

ANJA. No! You are big sister to them, spray of perfume, lolly, lot more chat, yes? Then you make top dollar, not pennies.

Yes? Yes, Cathy!

ANJA offers the cigarette to CATHY.

CATHY. I've given up.

ANJA. Yeah me too.

CATHY. We got time?

ANJA. Yeah. We deserve a break, fuck boss if he don't like it.

CATHY *takes the cigarette.* ANJA *lights her own cigarette, then lights* CATHY's.

Dirsas caurums.

CATHY. What does that mean?

ANJA. Asshole. He is.

Not like Georgiou. You know he likes you?

CATHY. Who, the one on the door, the bald one?

ANJA. Yes! 'Who's the hot bitch just start?' He said.

CATHY. He's a poet, is he?

ANJA. His cock is big.

CATHY. How do you know?

ANJA. Ha! Twice.

CATHY. You're seeing him then?

ANJA. No! He is so ugly and he smelled too much. I don't like.

CATHY. Get me his number then!

    Anja, you're gorgeous, yeah. Look at ya. You can do better than old Shrek out there.

ANJA. If I am stuck in Churchill House for six months I need something that feels like love.

CATHY. You been there six months?

ANJA. You still believe in thirty-three days?

CATHY. I'm on one hundred and twenty-two and counting.

ANJA. You know Karima? The nurse?

CATHY. Yeah.

ANJA. Two years. That's why she has depression.

CATHY. I can't be in that dive for two years!

ANJA. You try with three kids. All night they fight. Over the TV, who gets the pink plate, who goes on top bed.

CATHY. Dan ain't doing so good at school either. She's up at six, back at six. I never see her.

ANJA. Poor thing.

CATHY. I had a call from her teacher saying they're worried about her.

ANJA. I say thank God I am leaving.

CATHY. You're leaving? No! When?

ANJA. One month. Goodbye, Churchill, hello, Croydon.

ANJA gathers up her bag of perfumes, lollies, etc. Sets them down.

CATHY. You can't leave, Anja.

ANJA. Yes. Sorry.

CATHY. Who else am I gonna talk to? You're my… mate, aren't you.

ANJA. You come visit. Easy.

CATHY. How did you pull it off?

ANJA. I tell you, later. We should go back.

CATHY. Anja, wait, tell us.

ANJA. Okay. For assessment, the council need so much information. Credit score, doctor address and more and more. Always they lose letters, they send letters to wrong address. So you chase them tomorrow, then next day, next day.

I do this. I hear council say on phone. 'This one is such a pain in the arse.' They want rid of me. Now they are. Because I am big fucking pain in arse!

CATHY. You are!

ANJA. Cathy, you are like a cat in a bag saying, 'What a nice warm bag. I think I have a nice sleep.' Use this – (*Taps head.*)

Enter DALE. ANJA sees him and quickly stubs out her cigarette.

Shit.

DALE. There you are. I've been [looking for you]… what's all this then, girls eh?

ANJA. We have rest.

DALE. Come on, you ent paid for having a rest, luv. I've got toilets up there full of punters, floors soaking.

Come on, chop chop.

ANJA. We are coming. We need one minute.

DALE. No, mate, not a minute. Now yeah.

(*To* CATHY.) You normally take the piss on your first day, do ya?

CATHY. No, sorry –

ANJA. Is not her fault.

DALE (*to* CATHY). You just follow this one, do ya? Expert at taking the piss, this one.

ANJA. I work hard here.

DALE (*winking at* CATHY). Does she?

CATHY. Yeah.

ANJA. This only break I have. In six hours. It's not legal.

DALE *laughs*.

This is joke for you.

CATHY. Come on, Anja.

DALE. I'll tell you what's a joke, luv. It's your agency, taking on you lot.

ANJA (*mutters in Latvian*). *Dirsas caurums*.

DALE. What?

CATHY *laughs*.

You say something?

ANJA. No.

DALE. What did she say?

CATHY. Nothing, nothing.

DALE. You wanna say that in English? You've got to speak
English here, in – (*To* CATHY.) our country.

ANJA. This is bullshit.

DALE. Is it? It's too much to ask that you speak English?

We're allowing you to be here, paying you?

Giving you a nice house.

ANJA. Ha!

CATHY. You ain't seen it.

DALE. Saves you a bit though. Lets you send your benefits
back to Poland?

(*To* CATHY.) Feed her family of twenty kids.

ANJA *picks up her things*.

CATHY. I don't think –

ANJA. One point. I am from Latvia.

DALE. And where even is that?

ANJA. No one gives me house. We are stuck in shithole block.

CATHY. She's been in England ten years.

ANJA. I pay tax.

DALE. Of course you do, of course you do.

ANJA. So I have rights.

DALE. This is not your country. You're working for us. Now
pick up your shit, and get up into that toilet and do your job.

CATHY. There's no need for that. We're going back.

ANJA. No.

DALE. What?

ANJA. You heard.

DALE. Oh. You wanna go there, do ya?

CATHY. Anja, it ain't worth it.

ANJA. I don't need this.

DALE. No? You better than this? Better than being a bog troll?

ANJA *shrugs*.

CATHY. Anja, come on, mate!

ANJA. I have enough of this bullshit 'go home'. All the pissed
people say 'go home'.

DALE. So go then.

ANJA. I go.

CATHY. Anja, think about why you're doing this.

ANJA. Nah, fuck this.

DALE. Go on, luv, get your stuff and piss off, if you're too
good for us.

ANJA. Fine. *Dirsas caurums*.

Exit ANJA. DALE eyeballs CATHY challenging her to act.

CATHY. I'll go and get her. She don't mean what she said.

DALE. No, don't bother, I'm best rid.

Come on then, let's go.

CATHY *doesn't move*.

Don't you do what she's done. I need you up there, luv.

CATHY. You can't –

I know you think we're –

We're not [nothing].

DALE. But you said you were skint.

You got thirty seconds.

*Exit DALE. CATHY considers the bag of perfumes. What
should she do? She chooses to follow ANJA off.*

Scene Six

March 2016. A small room in Churchill House. Afternoon.

A mattress with two duvets. Piles of possessions in boxes.

DANIELLE *sits on a chair. She is wearing her school uniform. Her white shirt is ripped and has blood soaked into the front, and smears on the arms/cuffs where* DANIELLE *has wiped her bloody nose.*

CATHY *holds a bag of peas to the side of* DANIELLE*'s face.* ANJA *holds tissues for the blood.*

DANIELLE. That's freezing.

CATHY. Good, it'll take down the swelling.

Here. Press.

DANIELLE *presses the peas to her cheekbone.*

You know their names?

ANJA. Danielle, you know their names?

DANIELLE. I know one of them. The other four I didn't know.

CATHY. Four!

DANIELLE. Or five, I dunno. I couldn't tell.

ANJA. And who's the one you know?

DANIELLE. Just a girl I see at the bus stop.

CATHY. From a school round here?

DANIELLE. Look, you don't need to make a massive thing about it.

CATHY. Danielle, five girls have just jumped you.

DANIELLE. It's nothing, Mum, honestly.

CATHY *gives* ANJA *a look to leave.* ANJA *exits.*

CATHY. You ent gonna tell me this little cow's name?

DANIELLE. –

CATHY. They followed you off the bus?

DANIELLE. It was my fault.

CATHY. It was not.

DANIELLE. It was. They're sitting behind me and I'm on Snapchat to Eliydah and one of them grabs my phone. And they're like, 'You want it back?' and I'm like, 'Yeah,' and one says, 'Where's your school' and I'm like, 'London' and they all start going through my photos. Like laughing. And they see the ones of Eliydah and Samira and they're going, 'Who's that? How come you're friends with Pakis? Are they terrorists?' And I'm like, 'No, they're my best mates.' And Eliydah's Turkish anyway so – And they go, 'Your best mates are in Islamic State'. And so this girl Carmel grabs my bag and starts going through it pulling out all my stuff, like my tampons and everything, and she's like, 'There's a bomb in here,' and everyone on the bus screams. So I hit her.

CATHY. You hit her?

And that's why –

When you got off the bus –

DANIELLE. Yeah.

CATHY. Carmel, is it?

DANIELLE *realises she has given the name away.*

DANIELLE. You can't say anything.

CATHY. Dan, this is GBH. If I did this to someone I'd go to prison.

DANIELLE. I have to get the bus with them every day.

CATHY. It's a local school they go to?

DANIELLE. It don't matter if I you tell their school. And it don't matter if they all get suspended. Cos there'll be others to take their place. People hate us here, you know. All I hear is people saying that Churchill House is full of 'immigrants' and 'pikeys' and we're stealing their houses and taking their jobs.

This was supposed to be an emergency place. It's been months.

I can't breathe in this fucking room.

DANIELLE *looks out of the window.* CATHY *approaches her.*

CATHY. Here.

CATHY *puts her arms around* DANIELLE *and kisses her head.*

DANIELLE. I want to go home.

CATHY. I know, I know, luv. Me too.

Tell you what, we'll go out this weekend. Go round the shops.

DANIELLE. With what money?

CATHY. Don't worry about that. We'll get you a new coat.

DANIELLE. Don't bother. I ent going back to school.

CATHY. Dan, Dan, I know it ain't easy. But you gotta go, show em you ent scared.

DANIELLE. There's no point, Mum. Even if I get like twenty A-stars then ten A levels, I can't afford to go to uni. So I'll end up like –

CATHY. Me – ?

DANIELLE. I didn't mean it like that.

CATHY. You ent gonna be like me. Cos you are smart and beautiful and funny and you're gonna have the whole world at your feet, yeah.

DANIELLE. No I'm not.

CATHY. If it means I get loans and debts or whatever to get to through, I'll do that.

We gotta keep going, mate. Yeah?

I've been on to the council. They've got all the forms they need. And promising we'll get assessed by the end of next week. Then we'll go back home.

DANIELLE. That's a promise, is it?

CATHY. Yeah. By the end of the month, I promise.

Scene Seven

April 2016. London borough of Thames Wick housing office. Morning.

CATHY *is dressed in casual clothes and coat. Opposite the table from* SHANIA, *who is dressed in professional clothes. She has a printed document in front of her.* SHANIA *is bursting with enthusiasm.*

CATHY. Sorry I'm grinning. I must look stupid smiling like a Cheshire cat like –

Ha!

SHANIA *smiles.*

Nine months stuck in that –

I told Danielle, I showed her the message and she was –

I'm just properly –

SHANIA. As I said it was a positive decision.

CATHY. That's means we've got something?

SHANIA. This is your 184.

CATHY. Show us it then!

SHANIA *slides the pack over to* CATHY.

SHANIA. It's a two-bedroom maisonette in a purpose-built block. There's a kitchen, living room, built in cupboard units. It's carpeted throughout. Double glazing.

It's on the fifth floor.

CATHY. Don't matter.

SHANIA. Does that sound acceptable to you?

CATHY. Yeah – (*Re: photos.*) it looks quality.

SHANIA. It's only two years old so –

And ninety pounds a week.

CATHY. Cheap.

SHANIA. More money in your pocket.

It's not local though.

CATHY. But it's not Luton, is it!

Where is TE – ? The postcode.

SHANIA. Gateshead.

CATHY. Where's that, not round here is it?

SHANIA. No.

CATHY. Kent is it?

SHANIA. Gateshead is in Northumberland.

CATHY. Where's that near? You're gonna have to give me a town or something.

SHANIA. Newcastle?

CATHY. As in the brown ale? *with emphasis*

SHANIA. It has a keypad entry system.

CATHY. Newcastle? — *stand up*

SHANIA. The balcony overlooks a park. It's five hundred and fifty square foot. You're two miles from the city centre and the bus takes you into –

CATHY. Newcastle.

SHANIA. The city centre, in / twenty-five minutes.

CATHY. You are kidding me?

SHANIA. Can I put you down as a 'yes'?

CATHY. How many people do I know in Newcastle?

SHANIA. It's temporary accommodation, Ms Ward.

CATHY. And I'm supposed to just say yes?

SHANIA. This is our offer.

CATHY. I never said I wanted to move to Newcastle.

CATHY *pushes the documents back to* SHANIA.

Do I get to view it?

SHANIA. There's no viewings.

CATHY. So I can't even see it?

SHANIA. You either accept it now or not. If you take it, it'll be yours until you place a successful bid on a permanent property.

CATHY. And?

SHANIA. Every Friday you'll make a bid on a unit which matches your requirements and hopefully you'll be offered permanent accommodation.

CATHY. Here?

SHANIA. Or in a neighbouring borough.

CATHY. How long will that take?

SHANIA. It won't be immediate. You can expect to make about three to four hundred bids. So you're looking at waiting six or seven years.

CATHY. I've got to live in Newcastle for seven years? Danielle'll be twenty-two by then.

SHANIA. Okay.

CATHY. She won't be of school age. So I won't be in priority need.

SHANIA. You'd move into band three. Which is not priority need.

CATHY. And how long will it be till I get a place back home?

SHANIA. It depends how many people are in greater need.

CATHY. So I could bid every week for the rest of my life and never come back.

Beat.

Danielle's exams are in two months. Is she supposed to just get up and start at a new school?

SHANIA. Kids do adapt, in my experience.

CATHY. In your experience as a mum?

SHANIA. I don't have children.

CATHY. So you don't actually know what it's like –

For them to leave their home and their friends, their friends who are like everything to them at fifteen, who tell them who they are and make them feel special and popular and clever because they love each other to death.

SHANIA. You'll have each other.

CATHY. You really haven't had a teenage daughter.

SHANIA. I'm sure you'll make new friends, Mrs Ward.

CATHY. I'm forty-three.

SHANIA. That's still young.

CATHY. With all due respect, fuck off.

Beat.

SHANIA. I can't be spoken to like that. I'm going to get my supervisor.

Exit SHANIA. *Enter* PETER, *a senior housing officer.*
Re-enter SHANIA. — Sit down

PETER. Ms Ward –

My name is Peter Henshaw, I'm the Senior Supervisor here. I need you to remain calm.

PETER *indicates that they should sit. They sit.*

Ms Ward, other people aren't getting this offer. It's two bedrooms. Not a B&B. Not a hostel.

CATHY. You appreciate this is… it's a big move, yeah. It's big… it's not something I can just go 'yeah go ahead' to.

PETER. I know but –

CATHY. I'm the lucky one then. I should be grateful. I should be thankful.

SHANIA. Well.

CATHY. What do you mean, 'well'?

Where do you live?

SHANIA. That doesn't matter.

CATHY. It does because you just compared yourself to me.

SHANIA. I rent a flat.

PETER. Shania –

SHANIA. With my boyfriend.

CATHY. And you'll want to buy somewhere, get somewhere permanent?

PETER. Look this really isn't getting us / anywhere.

SHANIA. We can't afford it at the moment.

CATHY. And even though you and your boyfriend work full time you still can't afford anywhere. Because there aren't enough homes. And the ones there are are too expensive. /

PETER. Ms Ward /

SHANIA. We'll get on the ladder.

CATHY. You should be furious. But, no, you look at me, you both look at me and you think you're better than me. But I'll tell you this. If you lose your jobs and the benefits don't cover your rent and then you spend your savings and your family won't help then – (*Bangs the table.*) You're in arrears. And then you're out and then you're me.

Beat.

PETER. You sign in that box there.

CATHY. Here?

PETER. There.

CATHY *considers the form.*

CATHY. You got a pen?

PETER *pushes over a pen.*

I want to go home.

My dad.

Pause.

What if I don't sign this?

PETER. If you refuse an offer of Section 188 accommodation then you'll be deemed intentionally homeless. The council will relinquish its duty of care.

Your accommodation will be your responsibility.

CATHY. I don't want this. I want to go home.

PETER. Ms Ward, you have a daughter.

SHANIA. You need to do what's best for Danielle.

CATHY (*through her teeth*). I told you, do not tell me about being a mother.

SHANIA. This is a critical time for her.

CATHY (*struggling to control it*). I know. I know. I know.

(*Losing the battle.*) You don't tell me how to be a mother. YOU DO NOT EVER TELL ME ABOUT HOW TO BE A MOTHER.

YOU DON'T KNOW ME. YOU DON'T JUDGE ME.

CATHY *rips the offer document into pieces. She sobs.*

PETER. As there's a minor involved in this case, I'm duty bound to pass your file on to Social Services.

CATHY. What? WHAT?

You're not taking Danielle away from me. Is that what you want to do is it?

PETER. We can not allow a fifteen-year-old to sleep rough on the streets.

CATHY. Then give us somewhere to live.

PETER. We did. You rejected it.

SHANIA. I'm going to call the Social Services team now.

CATHY stands.

CATHY. No! You're not taking my daughter away from me.

You're not taking Danielle away.

As CATHY exits.

SHANIA. Wait, that's not what I'm –

Scene Eight

April 2016. BEX's house. Braintree, Essex. Early evening.

The garden. Inside the house is clean, beige and furnished in mid-range furniture. Sticks in jars. Framed photo prints. Distressed wood ornaments.

CATHY is in casual clothes. BEX in her coat, having been at work. BEX holds a mug out.

BEX. I'm not saying it's an issue, Cath.

CATHY. I should've closed the door.

BEX. It's not the door, I don't mind the patio door being open, it's this [cup] with your fag ends in it.

I'm not saying it's a problem, if you're staying here, just clean it up.

CATHY. Sorry, I forgot, Bex. The sun was out so I thought… I'd sit, feel the sun on my face. It's beautiful being in a garden.

BEX. You're making yourself at home, that's good.

You smoking again then?

CATHY. Not as such. A couple in the morning, sometimes –

BEX. Lot of ends in here.

I don't want Oli and Em seeing these. If they see you smoking then –

CATHY. I'll be a lesson for them. Don't smoke or you'll end up like Aunty Cath. Sleeping on sofas.

BEX. I didn't mean it like that. I remember what it was like for us. Mum and Dad both smoking, us coughing non-stop. It was disgusting.

CATHY. I can't remember that.

BEX. You do. Dad sitting in front of *Grandstand* with his coupons, puffing away. Yuck.

CATHY. We were happy though.

BEX. Cath, it was poky and dark and it was horrible. Best thing I ever did was get out of there.

CATHY. Thanks.

BEX. Not saying anything against you. That estate was fine, for you.

Braintree's different. The people here, they're different. They've got aspiration.

CATHY. Are you saying I don't?

BEX. No, Cath, course not. You've worked hard, haven't you? It's just a choice you made. When you married Glen.

CATHY. Choice?

BEX. You met Glen, I met Vic. I'm here, you're… you know.

CATHY. On your sofa.

BEX. Yeah.

Pause.

CATHY. We're grateful, Bex, you know that? We had nowhere else to go.

BEX. We're glad to help. We couldn't leave you in the rain. Like two drowned rats.

CATHY. I know we're in your way.

BEX. No, no! Your stuff's fine in the corner. Vic's getting used to it and he's fine now.

CATHY. Is he?

BEX. The kids don't mind sharing a room. We're all happy to have you here, we are.

It's not gonna be forever.

Till you're back on your feet.

Yeah.

CATHY. It's making a difference to Dan, you know. Having her own bed. Her own space. She's smiling, talking to me again.

BEX. Good. Good.

BEX *pauses, awkward.*

Vic was asking, he just mentioned… cos you know he'd do anything to help… He was wondering how long… you know.

Not wanting to sound like we're trying to [get rid of you].

Cos we're not.

CATHY. Oh.

BEX. You're not in the way.

CATHY. I don't know. Couple of… months?

BEX. Two months?

CATHY. Till Dan's exams are done? In June?

Is that okay, Bex?

Slight pause.

BEX (*unconvincing*). Yeah.

CATHY. We might be out of here sooner. I've found somewhere.

BEX. This your bidding?

CATHY. It's a little flat in Stratford. It's near home, it's got a couple of bedrooms, balcony, near a bus route. Eighteenth floor but... I'll show ya.

CATHY *opens* OLI's *laptop and begins booting it up and logging in to the webpage.*

This flat was fresh on yesterday so, there's a chance lot of people are gonna want it, but you never know. From the balcony you can see over the Olympic Park. Twenty minutes from Dan's school.

She is now on the website.

And... oh... it's gone.

BEX. But you said it was fresh on.

CATHY. Yeah but top of the list get priority.

BEX. Where are you on the list?

CATHY. The top five or six get a viewing. And if one of them wants it ...

BEX. Where are you in the list?

CATHY. We've sort of slipped down, cos of not being in the system. We're a hundred and twenty-eight.

BEX. You won't ever have got it then. How long are you gonna wait if you're a hundred and twenty-eight?

CATHY. They said six or seven years but never know.

BEX. Are you kidding me?

You can't live on this sofa for seven years.

Beat.

There's gotta be something else, surely?

CATHY. There's private. I've been calling agents all day, Bex. They find out you're on benefits, they hang up. They want two months rent upfront, deposit. That's about three, four grand.

BEX. Where are you gonna get that?

CATHY *looks at* BEX.

CATHY. What do think, Bex? If you could loan us, we could get somewhere near Dan's school. We could be out of here like – (*Clicks fingers.*) that. You could get your life back.

BEX. Three or four grand?

It's a lot of money, Cath. We've got bills. And the mortgage on this place.

CATHY. Can you ask Vic?

BEX. I know what'll he say, Cath. That you've made your bed.

You chose to stay in low-paid jobs. You chose to go on benefits. Why didn't you go to college, to better yourself.

CATHY *shoots* BEX *a furious look.*

CATHY. You know why, don't you?

BEX. I know you've looked after Dad, I know you have. But I've done my fair share.

CATHY. Visiting once a year?

BEX. I'm not local like you.

CATHY. But I am. So it falls on me. And I don't mind. Because that matters, to me.

Not playing golf all weekend. Or having a nice timeshare in the Algarve.

Pause.

BEX. You know when you knocked on the door, he said, 'Wait till she asks for money.'

CATHY. I don't want to, Bex. But I've got no one else to go to. You're family.

BEX. Family, yes. But not a bank.

CATHY. Please, Bex.

Where else do I go?

BEX. Go to Glen. He's the one who landed you in this mess. He's the one who gambled your life away. He should pay, not us.

CATHY. He's not seeing me like this.

BEX. He should. He should see what he's done.

CATHY. No, cos he don't get to see Dan. He lost that privilege.

Beat.

One loan. We could be back on our feet.

BEX. It's not like we haven't helped, Cath.

CATHY. Right –

BEX. We've cooked you dinner.

Let you watch what you want to watch on telly.

Not made a fuss if Dan leaves make-up all over the bathroom.

CATHY. I know, Bex.

BEX. Cos we've been thinking, you know, Oli's got his A levels in two months and he needs his own space to study.

And there's summer holidays coming up and they'll both be around more so –

CATHY. We can get out of your way.

BEX. You know what I'm saying, don't you, Cath?

This arrangement being –

Temporary.

CATHY. You're my sister, Bex.

BEX. I can't. Sorry.

Saturday. You can stay till next Saturday.

Scene Nine

May 2016. London. The living room of Steve's flat. 3 a.m.

A sofa. DANIELLE lies, reading her phone. Enter CATHY from a bedroom, timidly, wearing her bra, pants and a man's shirt. She holds a bath towel.

There should be as much air as we can stand between the exchanges here.

CATHY (*whispers*). Dan?

CATHY *crouches in front of* DANIELLE. DANIELLE *turns over, away from* CATHY.

Here.

It's cold in here.

No response. CATHY *hesitates before placing the towel over* DANIELLE*'s shoulders.* DANIELLE *throws it off.* CATHY *picks it up.*

Dan?

What you doing [on your phone]?

DANIELLE *turns her phone off.*

Long pause.

Here.

DANIELLE. I don't want it.

CATHY *looks around at all the piles of stuff that signify a single middle-aged man living alone.*

CATHY. You want a drink of water?

I might get a drink.

DANIELLE *doesn't respond.*

He said it's alright for us to stay.

Will you be alright out here?

That sofa don't look –

DANIELLE *shrugs.*

It's freezing.

CATHY *sits, looks around the room.*

DANIELLE. I left my new coat in the pub.

CATHY. No! Where?

DANIELLE *shrugs.*

I'll go back and get it in the morning.

CATHY *goes to the window and pushes the curtain open a crack.* DANIELLE *doesn't join in.*

I can see the Olympic Park.

The old flat's over there, see past the stadium.

You ever look at people's windows and wonder who's behind 'em? What's their life?

What did they do right?

DANIELLE. Can you shut up?

CATHY. I'm just saying.

DANIELLE. Just chatting shit.

There's no point you talking about 'em cos you're never gonna live in a house like that. Do you get that?

The only reason you're here is cos you got a bloke pissed in a pub.

Pause.

You know listening to your mum having sex is the most gross thing ever.

CATHY. We weren't having... I mean, we didn't –

DANIELLE. It sounded like it.

CATHY. We weren't.

DANIELLE. Whatever.

You found out his name yet?

CATHY. Steve. His name's Steve.

I told him my name was Julie.

DANIELLE. His flat stinks.

CATHY. He's alright though?

DANIELLE. If you like psychos.

CATHY. – ?

DANIELLE. He's got a knife. In the bathroom.

And you seen the names of his DVDs?

CATHY *picks up a DVD box, reacts.*

Good choice, Mum.

CATHY. He's been on his own.

DANIELLE (*sarcastic*). Obviously.

CATHY. He was in the army, in Basra. Two of his friends got shot dead by a kid. He lost his head and had to come home.

DANIELLE. Wow. He sounds like a total loser.

CATHY *picks up and holds out the towel.*

CATHY. It's a bed for you, eh? Here. Keep warm.

DANIELLE. You can tell him I don't want it.

CATHY. Dan?

DANIELLE. I wanna sleep alright.

CATHY. This ain't forever.

DANIELLE. That's all you ever say.

CATHY. It might seem like –

But I'll find somewhere tomorrow, somewhere we can stay. For a while.

DANIELLE. Another random man in a pub? Cos there's loads out there, Mum. We could stay somewhere different every night. It'll be like going travelling.

DANIELLE *turns over on the sofa and turns her phone on.*

CATHY. Maybe go back to that shelter. They might have room tomorrow.

DANIELLE. It was full of junkies.

CATHY. We'll get there early.

I'm sorry.

DANIELLE. Stop saying sorry. All you say is sorry. You've got to do something.

Go to the council.

CATHY. They've passed us on to Social Services. And you know what they'll do if –

DANIELLE. So… what then?

In the morning, when Sad Steve wakes up and he ain't pissed any more and he realised he's shagged some old woman. And her kid's sleeping on his sofa. What then? He'll ask us to move in for good?

What actually are we gonna do?

CATHY *hangs her head. She has no answers.*

CATHY. I'll call Anja. Maybe she'll have us back. Or Bobby.

DANIELLE. Or go to the hostel again.

CATHY. They wanted us to see a social worker, so no.

DANIELLE. We keep hiding from them then?

CATHY. I don't know.

DANIELLE. You're not supposed to say 'don't know'.

You're supposed to be my mum!

CATHY. Sssh!

DANIELLE *sobs.* CATHY *goes to console her.* DANIELLE *pushes her arm off.*

I don't… I mean I thought I… if I worked hard enough… that I'd… that we'd be okay.

I know I haven't been there all the time when you were –

And you must have wanted –

I know.

I am your mum.

I ain't perfect, God do I know that –

I should've got a better job, bought a place, found you a proper dad.

But I've tried… (*Taps heart.*) in here, so hard –

DANIELLE. My first exam is in three weeks.

DANIELLE *picks her phone up and walks to the opposite side to* CATHY. *She begins composing a text message.*

CATHY. What you doin'?

DANIELLE. Texting.

CATHY. Who?

DANIELLE. Doesn't matter.

CATHY. Dan? Who are you texting?

DANIELLE. Dad.

CATHY. No!

DANIELLE *continues texting*.

DANIELLE. See, tomorrow night, yeah, I wanna sleep in a bed. With pillows. And not in my clothes. And with my bag not under the covers, in case it's nicked.

I wanna wake up when I want. And have toast if I want or... I dunno... watch dumb stuff on telly. And not feel like... always having to be grateful to someone I don't know.

And not feel like... not feel like I'm nothing.

Pause.

CATHY. Okay, God, okay, fine.

DANIELLE. I'm gonna send it then.

DANIELLE *shows the phone to* CATHY.

Sent.

Scene Ten

July 2016. Ilford. A greasy spoon café. 2 p.m.

CATHY, DANIELLE *and* GLEN *stand over the table, nervous around each other.*

CATHY. You got your best clothes on then.

GLEN. This? Christmas present.

CATHY. Oh yeah, who from?

GLEN. Me. Sort of present to myself.

CATHY. It's nice. Suits you.

GLEN. Bit itchy round the collar but –

CATHY. I was sort of expecting you to be in tracky Bs.

GLEN. Tracky Bs. Listen to her.

CATHY. You look smart.

GLEN. Thought I'd make an effort for my girls, ha.

You alright, Danielle?

DANIELLE. Yeah.

GLEN. Yeah?

They sit.

CATHY. Danielle said you've been working?

GLEN. Yeah, on and off.

CATHY. You've got something now?

GLEN. Yeah yeah I've just been um working out me van, plumbing.

CATHY. So you're rolling in it.

GLEN. I wouldn't say that but –

CATHY. You're still in that chicken place in Ilford?

GLEN. Thank you, Cath, the flat's still above a Chicken Cottage.

CATHY. You been there a while.

GLEN. Yeah.

CATHY. But you're doing alright. You got enough for that shirt.

GLEN. Like I say, it's itchy but –

I got jeans too. Teekers. Forty quid off.

CATHY. Well done.

GLEN (*unsure*). Thanks.

You look very smart too, Cath.

CATHY. Ha, no I don't, Glen. It's Bex's. I haven't washed it for three days.

GLEN. I've got a cold so… you could both stink and I wouldn't notice. Ha.

You decided what you want, Danielle?

DANIELLE *looks to* CATHY.

Have whatever you like, Dan.

DANIELLE (*to* CATHY). What are you gonna have?

GLEN. There's full Englishes here. There's omelettes, sausage, porridge. Cath?

CATHY. I'm not that hungry.

GLEN. It's near two o'clock, you not starving? We should make this special. When's the last time we got together? Go the full works. They got teas or coffees or if you want one of them smoothies, Dan. We can't just do toast. I don't ever get a call out the blue from you so –

DANIELLE. Dad, the reason we're not getting anything is cos WE'VE GOT NO MONEY.

We're homeless. Alright?

Beat.

GLEN. You what?

What, like –

CATHY. No not –

GLEN. On the streets?

DANIELLE. Basically yeah.

If we don't find somewhere then yeah we are –

GLEN. Not like 'on the streets' –

DANIELLE. Yeah, really, Dad.

GLEN *looks incredulous at* CATHY.

GLEN. So what are you, er… you looking for –

I would but –

I haven't got a lot of room, to –

CATHY. We don't want to stay with you, Glen.

GLEN. So – ?

CATHY *hesitates*.

DANIELLE. Go on.

CATHY. It's that we erm… we wanted to /

GLEN. To what? What's going on? I thought this was a 'clear the air' sort of thing.

CATHY. Glen, we haven't heard from you in nine years why would –

DANIELLE. Mum!

CATHY. Why would we want to clear the air?

GLEN. I dunno, do I? You tell me what you're here for then. Cath?

CATHY. It's just that… we've stayed with my sister and my friend but that didn't… and I don't get my benefits till the end of /

DANIELLE. Dad, Mum's trying to ask for money.

GLEN. From me?

CATHY. Yes, from you, Glen.

GLEN. Like what you got in mind?

CATHY. A loan. For a room.

DANIELLE. A hotel.

CATHY. Or even a B&B or something.

GLEN. How much are they?

CATHY. About fifty quid.

GLEN. A month?

CATHY. Not a month, Glen.

    Doesn't have to be, it could anywhere, just a roof. Near
    Dan's school.

GLEN. For how long?

CATHY. Till she's done her exams. In June.

GLEN. No, I mean how long do you want me to pay?

CATHY. My child benefit comes through in a week.

DANIELLE. It's not long, Dad.

GLEN. A week. That's what – (*Counts it out.*) three hundred
    and fifty quid.

CATHY. Maybe you could just stop buying shirts for a bit.

GLEN. You think this cost a carpet? Primark, mate.

CATHY. Glen, I'm asking. Please don't make us beg. I'm
    asking you to lend us the money to keep us off the streets.

    Pause.

DANIELLE. Dad?

GLEN. Dan, get our orders in, yeah? Full Englishes.

    He takes a twenty-pound note from his pocket and gives it to
    DANIELLE.

DANIELLE. Okay.

    Exit DANIELLE

CATHY. So?

    Pause.

GLEN. It's tough, Cath.

    I went out bought this shirt yeah I wanted to make you think,
    'Yeah he's doing all right he's getting on he's changed he

ain't losing,' you know, that ain't me no more and it ain't but... but, Cath, I ain't, I can't sit here play the big bling shit cos I'm... I've got nothing, Cath.

CATHY. You've got a job.

GLEN. And rent. A grand a month for a place that stinks of fried chicken.

CATHY. You've not saved anything?

GLEN. I ain't totally out of old habits, you know.

CATHY. Why? You've been on your own. The only person you've had to spend money on is you.

I have never got child support from you.

GLEN. I've wanted to.

CATHY. I have paid for every uniform, every school trip, her pocket money, clothes, phones, tickets, shoes, trips with school. For fifteen years.

I have worked three jobs. I have scrubbed out drains with these hands. I have done extra shifts till 5 a.m. I spent nothing on me. I have people look down on me like I'm shit. And talk to me like I'm nothing. I have done that because I am not nothing. Cos I have her.

Where were you?

Enter DANIELLE.

GLEN. I paid for stuff. Them first five years I was there.

CATHY. You weren't though, was you, Glen. You were in the bookies, always promising, promising to win it back.

GLEN. I was there.

CATHY. You was drunk, or asleep.

You've had fifteen years to be a decent father and this is your moment.

Please.

GLEN (*mutters, trying to keep controlled*). You fuckin' –

> You know why I have a flutter? Cos / when them horses are running towards that line.

DANIELLE. Look, the two of you, shut up. Shut up.

GLEN. I can't fuckin' [hack this].

> *Exit* GLEN. DANIELLE *shoots* CATHY *a look*.

DANIELLE. Why are you winding him up?

CATHY. Sorry, he just –

> I know he's your dad and you want him to be nice, some sort of loveable rogue. But there's a fine line between being a rogue and a cunt. And he is a cunt.

> *Enter* GLEN. *He puts a can of Coke on the table.*

GLEN. Listen, money-wise… I can't… I just ent got nothing. I honestly haven't. And I know that makes me a prick but –

> I got a sofa, like. And there's room –

CATHY. For tonight.

GLEN. Yeah but, it's not like there's loads of –

CATHY. It's alright.

GLEN. What I mean is, like, there's probably room for one person.

CATHY. I don't mind sleeping on the floor.

GLEN. Right. Right. Erm… it's sort of difficult cos… I'm kinda seeing someone, a woman sort of thing. At the moment so –

> And she gets like, she might –

DANIELLE. Mum's gotta come too.

GLEN. Yeah yeah. But it's kind of –

DANIELLE. Dad.

GLEN. Maybe Danielle comes tonight and we'll see.

CATHY. Where do I go?

DANIELLE. Dad?

GLEN *gets fifty pounds in different notes from his pocket and puts it on the table.*

GLEN. For tonight.

CATHY *takes the money.*

What do you think, Dan, you wanna come to mine?

You can get to school easy from Ilford, can't ya?

CATHY. No.

GLEN. It makes sense.

CATHY. No.

GLEN. Come on, Cathy, you know it does.

CATHY. I don't care. I'm not leaving her.

GLEN. And I ain't having my daughter sleeping on the streets. Cos that's what we're talking about here. You and Dan begging with the junkies and –

DANIELLE. I don't wanna sleep rough, Mum.

CATHY. You won't, luv.

DANIELLE. I've been sleeping on sofas and cushions for three months.

GLEN. She's not safe with you.

CATHY. She is safer with me than she could ever be with you.

GLEN. She's always been safe round mine, come on!

Beat.

CATHY. What do you mean 'always'.

GLEN. Um –

CATHY. Dan?

Pause.

GLEN. Sometimes Dan's come round, stayed over.

CATHY. No no no, no she hasn't.

GLEN. –

DANIELLE. –

CATHY. You've never stayed at his, have you, Dan?

DANIELLE. –

CATHY. You have never stayed at his, have you?

Not without telling me.

You haven't stayed at your dad's, have you?

DANIELLE *nods.*

DANIELLE. When I've been staying at Eliydah's.

CATHY. That's once a month.

CATHY *sits still, processing the information.*

DANIELLE. I was gonna say something but –

CATHY *stands, in tears.*

Mum – ?

I would have told you but I knew you wouldn't like it.

I just wanted to know.

CATHY *steps towards the exit.*

Please?

Mum…

CATHY *is at the exit.*

Love you.

CATHY *shakes her head in response and exits.*

Scene Eleven

September 2016. A bus station. London. Morning.

CATHY *sits on a plastic chair in a portakabin.* KAREN, *middle-aged, in a high-vis London bus driver's coat. She hands* CATHY *a mug of tea.*

KAREN. I can't remember if you said sugar so I put one in. Thought you might like the energy, you know. That alright? Quite strong.

My other half makes it terrible. Puts the bag in then whips it out after ten seconds. Like dishwater it is.

But that one, that's a decent brew, that. That alright?

CATHY. Thanks.

KAREN. You're welcome.

They drink their tea. An awkward silence between them.

You know, most mornings, end of shift we got someone sat here. All sorts. Men, women, kids sometimes, you wouldn't think but yeah kids, twelve, fourteen. Artem had one who was eight. Bit of a surprise that was.

Polish, lot of Polish. Bangladeshis. Romanians.

Back and forward on the buses. All night. Get on, get off, get on, get off.

How long you been doing it for?

CATHY. A month.

KAREN. Always on the 25?

CATHY *nods her head softly.*

Yeah, 25's a good bus. Nice straight route. Not so many hills.

Pause.

Get nasty sometimes, you lot, don't ya?

CATHY. – ?

KAREN. You fight over the seats, don't you? To get to that back one over the engine, where it's warmest.

CATHY. You said 'you lot'.

KAREN. Did I, oh sorry. I didn't mean –

I don't mean you're a tramp. You're not, you're –

I don't wanna say homeless but –

CATHY. Homeless.

KAREN. Yeah it is homeless, that's the word, is it.

What do you normally do now then?

Get food?

CATHY *nods*.

The one at Victoria? Yeah, I've heard that's a good one. Do hot stuff there, don't they? Yeah.

What about then, after that?

CATHY. There's a centre. I get washed. I play cards.

KAREN. There's blokes who are builders. Cleaners.

There's a few girls who work in the stores on Oxford Street. I kid you not. M&S one old girl was working in. That's right.

So why the 25? Of all the buses.

CATHY. Ilford.

KAREN. That where you lived, is it?

CATHY. My daughter.

KAREN. You still see her?

CATHY *shakes her head*.

Speak to her?

CATHY *shakes her head*.

When's the last time you saw her then?

CATHY. In a café.

KAREN. You look out from that bus window, don't ya? Just in case you see her.

Thought so.

CATHY. I saw her. Last week.

KAREN. Yeah?

CATHY. She was at the bus stop. She didn't look up.

I was going to wave, tap on the window.

I had it rehearsed in my head what it'd be like if I –

What I'd say. And she'd say. And we'd –

But I didn't.

She was with her friends.

KAREN. Good she's got friends.

CATHY. She's sixteen. Had her birthday, July. She's done her exams.

KAREN. She'll have done good, I know.

KAREN rummages around in her pocket for her phone.

Here.

KAREN takes out her phone.

Call her.

CATHY shakes her head.

Go on, why not?

CATHY shakes her head.

I got six hundred free minutes on this. I don't use 'em. My other half only got us this so she can nag us anytime she likes.

Call her. Please. Call her.

CATHY. She won't want that.

KAREN. You know that? For sure?

KAREN *holds out the phone again.* CATHY *picks at the cup.*

CATHY. I should go.

KAREN. You don't have to –

CATHY. Thanks for the tea.

KAREN. Stay for another cup?

CATHY *stands.*

Here, I never got your name.

CATHY. It doesn't matter.

KAREN. To me it does.

CATHY. Julie.

KAREN. Julie?

CATHY. No, it's not. It's Cathy.

KAREN. Cathy? I'm Karen.

KAREN *holds out his hand for shaking.* CATHY *considers. Shakes it.*

You're doing alright, Cathy.

You are. This world kicks us if we trip.

Not everyone's gonna kick you.

This – (*The phone.*) is here whenever I'm here.

And I'm always here.

Scene Twelve

September 2016. East London. Morning.

CATHY *stands in a puffy jacket and jeans. It's dirty and her hair is different.* DANIELLE *wears a pair of fashionable black-rimmed glasses and coat.*

She takes her earphones out, turns off the music and wraps them around the phone.

DANIELLE. I didn't know if this was the place you meant.

CATHY. Yeah. Yeah it is.

Slight pause.

You look well.

DANIELLE. Yeah, you too.

Pause.

I didn't know it was [you].

I didn't recognise your number, on my phone.

CATHY. It wasn't mine.

DANIELLE. Eliydah said I shouldn't pick up. She said it was probably just a prank call.

Slight pause.

CATHY. I'm glad you did.

Beat.

DANIELLE. Look, I know you're gonna ask about my exams. I messed 'em up so don't say anything, okay.

CATHY. You've got the results?

DANIELLE. Yeah.

CATHY. And – ?

DANIELLE. Mum.

CATHY *looks at* DANIELLE, *studies what she's wearing.*

CATHY. Those glasses are nice.

DANIELLE. They're just like… they're not cos I can't…

DANIELLE *takes the glasses off.*

CATHY. I've got a flat now.

DANIELLE. Yeah?

CATHY. I've been in this refuge and they helped, helped me sort a place. In West Bromwich.

I'm moving next week.

DANIELLE. West Bromwich?

CATHY. Nearer than Newcastle. Means I'll be able to see ya. More.

DANIELLE. –

CATHY. That'll be good, yeah?

DANIELLE. How often?

CATHY. All the time if you –

DANIELLE. –

CATHY. Or maybe.

You could come and see it. First.

And if you think –

Maybe you could, we could –

DANIELLE. Hang out?

CATHY. Yeah.

DANIELLE. In West Bromwich?

CATHY. Or I could come to you?

DANIELLE. And do what?

CATHY. Whatever you want. Shops?

DANIELLE. – ?

CATHY. Today if you want, if you haven't got –

DANIELLE. I'm going out with Eliydah's mum and her later. We're going down Southend.

You know I'm living with them?

CATHY. No. I thought you were still with your dad?

DANIELLE. That weren't… it didn't work out. Don't say, 'I told you so', but –

CATHY. But.

DANIELLE. He was –

CATHY. Drinking?

DANIELLE (*nods*). Then saying stuff about you. And me. And he, after a while he was making me feel, like worse, like I was –

Like this – (*Makes small gesture with finger and thumb*.) big.

CATHY. That's his –

Dan. You aren't. You don't need him to tell you nothing.

Pause.

DANIELLE. You still hate us then?

CATHY. What? When have I ever – ?

DANIELLE. Cos of, in the café.

CATHY. That? No! You was well within your rights. You had to get a roof over your head, didn't you.

DANIELLE. Yeah but –

I was –

I've been thinking about it, going over it, when you walked out and –

On my way here I was all shaking, I didn't know what you'd be like. I was thinking of all the things you might say –

Cos I've been thinking ever since it happened, that you must think I'm selfish.

CATHY. No.

DANIELLE. I just let you go.

CATHY. It was the right thing. I don't hate you.

DANIELLE. No?

CATHY. Come here, you silly arse.

>CATHY *opens her arms.* DANIELLE *is cautious, still not sure. She hesitates, then takes* CATHY*'s embrace.*

DANIELLE. You smell.

CATHY. Yeah. Sorry.

You wanna go round the shops then?

DANIELLE. I'm going to Southend, aren't I.

CATHY. Tomorrow then?

DANIELLE. Soon.

CATHY. Westfield?

DANIELLE. All right.

CATHY. They ain't got great shops in West Bromwich, Dan.

DANIELLE. Where's West Bromwich?

CATHY. Left of Birmingham.

We should set a date. When we can hang out.

DANIELLE (*unconvincing*). Yeah.

CATHY. Yeah.

DANIELLE. I better go. We're getting the train.

CATHY. I'll call you about Westfield.

DANIELLE. You got no phone.

CATHY. From a payphone then. I'll give you a call and –

>DANIELLE *moves to exit.*

You are gonna come and visit me, aren't you?

DANIELLE. I gotta go.

Beat.

CATHY. Dan? Tell me what you got. Your exams.

DANIELLE. I told you. I messed them up.

CATHY. I don't mind.

DANIELLE. It ain't all As like you wanted.

CATHY. I don't mind.

DANIELLE. Okay.

I got As in Biology and Maths, Bs in Physics, Religious studies and Chemistry, C in English Language, Ds in History and IT and Es in English Lit and French.

CATHY. Oh, Dan, that's so [good].

DANIELLE. Samira got like nine A-stars and a B, so yeah.

CATHY. It's enough for college?

DANIELLE. Yeah. I'm starting at Tower Hamlets College next week. Doing a BTEC.

Pause.

I really better [leave] –

CATHY. Yeah.

DANIELLE *goes to exit.*

Dan, tell me again. Your results.

DANIELLE. Two As, three Bs and two / Cs and –

CATHY. No, I wanna hear them one by one.

DANIELLE. – ?

CATHY. Do it for me, one by one.

DANIELLE. An A, an A, a B, a B, a B, a C, a D, a D, an E, an E.

CATHY (*slowly, relishing*). An A, an A, a B, a B, a B, a C, a D, a D, an E, an E.

CATHY *smiles*.

End.

Other Titles in this Series

A Nick Hern Book

Cathy first published in Great Britain as a paperback original in 2016 by Nick Hern Books Limited, The Glasshouse, 49a Goldhawk Road, London W12 8QP, in association with Cardboard Citizens

Cathy copyright © 2016 Ali Taylor

Ali Taylor has asserted his right to be identified as the author of this work

Cover image: Design by Well Made Studio. Copyright © Cardboard Citizens

Designed and typeset by Nick Hern Books, London

Printed in the UK by Mimeo Ltd, Huntingdon, Cambridgeshire PE29 6XX

A CIP catalogue record for this book is available from the British Library

ISBN 978 1 84842 628 3

Woodland
CARBON
www.woodlandcarbon.co.uk
NICK HERN BOOKS
Printed on Carbon Captured paper